The Lonely Grave

How a Homestead Murder
In South Dakota Brought
Closure 100 Years Later

Sue Speck

The Lonely Grave

How a Homestead Murder
in South Dakota Brought
Closure 100 Years Later

Copyright © 2026 Sue Speck

ISBN 979-8-992997-4-9

The true story of a brutal homestead murder and how it still impacts a family and a community more than a century later.

All rights reserved. No part of this book may be used or reproduced in any manner without written permission from the author except in the case of brief quotations in articles or reviews.

Printed in the United States of America

Dedicated to
my parents
Robert and Leona
and to my brother Gary.

My sincere thanks
to the people of Buffalo County
and to the members of Duncan Church,
especially Ellen Speck and Kathy Yost
for their gracious help and insight.

This non-fiction book is based on
court documents, including
trial transcripts, land deeds and
weather records, historical research,
settler's written memories and letters,
old newspaper articles and
interviews with living people
who have connections to the case.

Table of Contents

Part 1 Life and Murder on the Plains
Chapter 1
Chapter 2
Chapter 3
Chapter4
Chapter 5
Chapter 6
Chapter 7
Chapter 8
Chapter 9
Chapter 10
Chapter 11
Chapter 12

Part 2 Life After the Trial
Chapter 13

Part 3 A Century Later
Chapter 14
Chapter 15

Part 4 Living with the Past
Chapter 16

Part 5 Historical Perspective
Chapter 17
Chapter 18

Note on the Name Spelling

Part 6 The Story Behind the Story

About the Author
Acknowledgements
Endnotes

The photo on the cover

is the actual

grave and cemetery.

Part 1

Life and Murder on the Plains

Chapter 1

He thinks about it most in the spring and summer when he's out working in his fields and pastures.

Richard Sinkie still farms in Eden township, as his great grandfather did before him in the 1880's during the pioneer days of Dakota Territory.

All land comes with a history.

He grew up hearing about the hardships the pioneers experienced as they tried to cultivate this untamed land. The strain of solvency, the helplessness of being at the whims of the weather and epidemics, the sheer struggle for survival and the shadows that can bring.

When typhoid struck his Great Grandfather H.J. Sinkie's homestead, his great grandmother lay on what appeared to be her deathbed for days. H.J., who had already lost everything in a prairie fire in 1889, prayed to God, "Take all I have, but save my wife."

His wife survived, but a bout with diphtheria in 1898 took two of their sons. The body of one of them still lies in a grave on their original farm today.[1]

Richard Sinkie also grew up hearing about a murder on another farm his family bought later in the homestead days. In the pasture where he mows hay each year. The pasture with a dark history.

Every year, he drives his tractor and mower past the few remaining scattered remnants of the old house, the scene of the crime.

Back and forth. His tractor pulls his mower across the pasture.

Back and forth. The mower swishes through the meadow.

Back and forth. The whizzing blades whir through the stems.

Back and forth. The sharp sickles slice the grass to the ground.

And every year he wonders why it happened. How could anyone do that?

Summertime rolls around again. Time to cut hay again. He fires up his International Harvester brand mower, the same old reliable farm machine he's used for decades.

He turns the key. The mower vibrates as it starts, then it whirs and clangs and clatters and jangles. The clamorous sounds continue to rise until they eventually reach a crescendo of a loud squeal. A pitch so piercing that it sounds like a screech.

A screech.

A shriek.

Is that how it ended?

All those years ago?

Chapter 2

Richard Sinke's ancestors, like millions of other pioneers, were beckoned west by the promise of free land under the Homestead Act of 1862, romanced by the prospect of owning their own piece of America and making a living off their labors.

Settlers hungry for an opportunity at a new life rode covered wagons pulled by horses or oxen, took trains and even walked to places like Dakota Territory as it was called before it became the state of South Dakota.

It was a dirty, dusty, often treacherous journey over a prairie largely devoid of trees, prone to drought, dust storms and grass fires in dry seasons, and invasions of grasshoppers obliterating crops with their miniscule but relentless chewing jaws.[2]

Temperatures could hit over 100 degrees in the summer and plummet to deadly cold temperatures in the winter with unpredictable blizzards that could create unconquerable white-out conditions if you were caught outside when the storms hit.

Nonetheless, they came.

For a small filing fee of $10, plus other fees that added up to $18 in total, they could claim 160 acres, which was a quarter of one section of land.

The settlers could earn clear title to the quarter if they fulfilled the conditions of the Homestead Act by cultivating at least 10 acres, building a dwelling at least 12 feet by 14 feet and living on the land for five years.[3]

Simple enough. But not so easy. Only about half of the homesteaders who filed a claim were able to reach the five-year milestone to earn full title to their land.[4]

Their homes were often a hastily constructed one-room house made of lumber if you could find it or afford it, a dugout carved out of a hillside, or a sod house built of cut blocks of grass covered earth that were stacked up like bricks. When the wind howled, it could shake the claim shanties and blow through the cracks in the walls that settlers tried to block with rags, mud, newspaper and tar paper.[5]

When coal or wood wasn't available, as it often wasn't, fuel consisted of strands of twisted hay or dried buffalo and cow dung: "cow chips," which H.J. Sinkie called "hill and valley coal."[6]

But at the end of those hard five years, the homesteaders had "proved up" their claim, proved their worth, and proved that they could survive an experience that could make you or break you.

Chapter 3

When Daniel and Sarah Kelley arrived in central Dakota Territory in the last decades of the 19th century, railroads were expanding across the plains with trains co-existing alongside the horse-drawn wagons and buggies that most people were still using for transportation.

It was ten years after the gold rush had started in the Black Hills, a period that ushered in the Great Dakota Boom when settlers flocked to Dakota Territory and crops were producing bountiful yields.[7]

Around 1887, the Kelleys staked their claim for 160 acres in the center of the state in Buffalo County, a county created in 1864 and named for the buffalo that roamed this part of the Midwest for thousands of years.

It's semi-arid ground with long, rolling hills that were gouged out by glaciers during the Ice Age and part of the geological Plateau du Coteau du Missouri. The Missouri River, flanked by its rugged bluffs, flows southward along Buffalo County's western boundary, where the Native Americans hunted bison before the homesteaders had ever heard of this land.[8]

By the time the Kelleys arrived, the tension between the settlers and the Native Americans had dissipated, resolved with guns, force and treaties, and the Native Americans in central Dakota Territory had been relocated to the Crow Creek Reservation.[9]

The Kelleys found a piece of land north of Gann Valley, which is the Buffalo County seat. It's said to be the smallest county seat in the nation. Gann Valley went through its time of growth as homesteaders swarmed into the area. Today, the town proper only boasts about a dozen residents.

By the time Dan and Sarah Kelley staked their claim in Eden Township, enough homesteaders had moved to the area so that they had neighbors, a school nearby and a church just a few miles away.

Along with their children, John and Mary, who was nicknamed Mamie, Dan and Sarah set up farming near the Buffalo County - Hand County line. Their eldest son Charles, who was about twelve years older than his younger siblings, had moved to California.

They built a small sod house, then quickly expanded to a bigger wood house with a living area, a kitchen, a pantry, bedrooms and even closets and a storm shed. The foundation was constructed of sturdy, solid rocks.

To neighbors who were still living in sod houses like Richard Sinkie's ancestors, it looked almost palatial.

To Dan and Sarah Kelley, who built it after immigrating to the United States from Ireland and Scotland, it was their dream home.

The Kelleys dug a well with a windmill nearby and built a barn. They broke sod for crops. They ran cattle and horses. It was the quintessential all-American farm and ranch.

From all appearances, the Kelley homestead was prosperous. They were doing well in this rugged land. Their son John also started a well-digging business, a much-needed service and a practical supplement to the farm income, which rose and fell with the patterns of the weather.

Nature was generous in the beginning, providing enough rainfall to sustain thriving crops and lush grassland for the livestock to graze. In fact, there were bumper crops at first. The good times were rolling as more wagons rolled in during "The Great Dakota Boom."[10]

Farmers grew comfortable enough to expand and buy the new equipment that was being invented and advancing farming, including tougher plows that were more efficient at turning the stubborn sod on the Great Plains. Bank loans were often granted based simply upon expectations of a good harvest in the fall.[11]

But, in an ever-changing environment, fortunes can change too. A farmer can often survive a year of drought, but if your sustenance and source of income evaporate for an extended period, things can turn.

And it doesn't take very long.

By the late 1880's, the ten-year long Dakota Boom was beginning to turn into a Dakota bust, ushering in nearly ten years of frequent drought conditions. Especially severe drought lingered between the years from 1889 to 1894.[12]

Scorching, relentless winds shriveled crops. Water sources for cows and horses were drying up.

Gann Valley resident Ellsworth E. Dye wrote, "Hot winds almost like blasts from a red hot furnace continued day after day. Vegetation burned and withered and there was... ...no hay nor crops of any kind and these conditions brought about hardship and suffering." [13]

There were massive crop failures in 1890. Wheat that had been producing more than six bushels per acre fell to one bushel per acre and that was in the James Valley, known for its fertile farmland and normally abundant rainfall.[14]

Following the 1890 crop failure, Ellsworth E. Dye wrote that the state and the county furnished seed grain to the needy applicants and appeals were sent to other states to help the "Dakota sufferers" to prevent starvation.

No crops equals no income and no food for a farmer and the communities that depend on the mutually beneficial relationship. In 1894, conditions were so bad that some counties even abandoned efforts to collect taxes.[15]

At the other extreme was the winter.

Two harsh winters in 1886 and 1887 preceded a catastrophic blizzard in 1888. Named the "The Children's Blizzard," it hit on a day that started out deceptively bright and warm. By 9 a.m., a howling, raging mega storm with temperatures as low as 40 degrees below zero steamrolled over the Plains, stranding anyone who was caught in it, including school children trying to make it home.

An estimated 500 people died in the blizzard. Losses to the homesteaders' livestock were massive.[16]

The winter of 1896 was called the winter of deep snow. Blizzards blew through the winter season and didn't let up until the middle of March in 1897.[17]

By the 1890's, banks were beginning to foreclose on some of the farmland that had been mortgaged to buy seed to plant crops, buy more property or to purchase equipment and make improvements.

To compound the problems, a financial crisis hit in 1893 causing a nationwide depression. Many settlers who couldn't pay their mortgage or simply couldn't survive off their land even if they weren't in debt abandoned their homesteads and headed back to where they came from.[18]

Through all of this though, the Kelleys seemed to be holding their own in this unforgiving environment. No signs of trouble here. Solid as the rocks upon which their home was built.

In fact, in 1896, Dan Kelley was able to buy another quarter of land at a foreclosure sale.

And, by 1900, conditions began to turn around, leading to a prolonged period of good crops and prosperity in "The Golden Age of Agriculture."[19]

Chapter 4

The morning of February 23, 1905, dawned cold, but tolerable. It was a welcome change from temperatures that had been especially brutal in the first half of the month, dipping down to 47 degrees below zero in the area.[20]

John Kelley arose early that Thursday to get ready to go to Spring Lake with his business partner in his well digging business. He hitched his wagon to his team of horses and talked with John Hanson for a while by the windmill. The two left around 9 a.m. His parents were still inside the house.[21]

About two and one-half hours later, at the Eden Township schoolhouse that was a quarter mile away from the Kelley home, teacher Effie Forbes looked out the window.

She saw Dan Kelley slowly walking to the school in the winter chill. His head was down. His hand was clenched to his breast.

He knocked on the door and asked the teacher if he could speak with one of the Hoobler boys. He wanted them to fetch their mother and bring her to his house because his wife was dead.

"I asked if she was really dead," Effie said. "And he said, yes and she gone down cellar after potatoes and had fallen and was killed."

"He was out to the barn doing chores and came to the house and heard her groaning in the cellar."

Harold Hoobler rushed to get his mother and Effie Forbes offered to go to the Kelley home to help. Effie was not well acquainted with Dan and Sarah Kelley, but she had visited with John and Mamie Kelley, who were closer to her age.

Dan accepted her offer to help, then turned and left the schoolhouse and walked back home.

The teacher gave instructions to her students about what to do in her absence, then hurried with one of the students to the Kelley house. Dan met them at the door of the storm shed when they arrived.

Effie walked into the house and saw Sarah Kelley lying on the floor about five feet from the stove and near a trap door that led to the cellar.

The 56-year-old was lying on her back with her hands folded across her waist. She was wearing an "everyday" dress, as Effie described it, and a black bonnet on her head that covered her hair, which was described as being brown or red and flecked with gray.

Effie noticed that Sarah was wearing men's socks on her feet.

Sarah Kelley looked immaculate. Not even a drop of blood visible from a distance.

Effie walked over to Sarah's body. At first glance, she saw that Sarah had a gash over her right eye. She also saw some of the potatoes Sarah was going to prepare for dinner.

"On the east side of the stand was a common kind of milk pail about half full of water and had peeled potatoes in it, enough for a good meal for three or four men," Effie said later.

By this time, other neighbors were arriving to help, including H.J. and Bertha Sinkie, Annas Cunningham and W.A. Hoobler and his wife.

W.A. Hoobler checked the pulse on Sarah's wrist. "I took hold of her wrist, and the wrist was warm, but there was no pulse there."

"I asked him how it happened and he said she must have struck on the (water) tank in the cellar," Hoobler said.

Dan told his neighbors that he had lifted his wife out of the cellar to try to help her, but she had only breathed for a couple more minutes before taking her last breath on the kitchen floor.

As was the norm in the days before easily accessible funeral homes and morticians, the neighbors began to prepare the woman's body and dress her in clothes appropriate for a wake and a funeral, which were often held in the homes of the deceased. They made sure the house was tidy too.

Good neighbors doing what they could for a grieving husband who had just lost his wife to a terrible accident.

Dan found two boards to place his wife's body on while she was washed and prepared. Dan, Effie Forbes, H.J. Sinkie and Mrs. Thorn picked up Sarah and placed her on the makeshift table.

A closer look revealed bruises on her upper lip and two scratches on her chin. There were gashes on the skull and on her forehead and the sides of her face.

Yet, despite the wounds, there were no visible signs of blood except for a few drips at the back of her head.

More injuries than one would expect from a single fall. So many wounds. So little blood.

And it appeared that someone had already cleaned Sarah Kelley and changed her clothes.

A grieving husband who found his dying wife and couldn't bear to see her that way or someone else? After all, Dan said he was in barn.

So many questions starting to form.

But it was becoming apparent that Sarah Kelley had not died from a simple fall where she had struck her head on one object.

Through the initial shock of it all, the neighbors continued caring for Sarah Kelley's body. She had to be prepared for a proper burial. It was a matter of compassion and respect. It was the least a community could do for a neighbor in a time of tragedy.

Chapter 5

The more they cleaned, the more they saw.

The wounds were deep. Many to the bone. Some straight. Some curved. A jagged wound where part of the skin on her skull had been torn off by the force of the blows.

Closer inspection revealed three blows to the head, two very deep in the back of the head. In addition to the scratch on her chin and marks on her lip, she also had wounds by her hairline. There were marks on her neck as well.

So far, the only blood visible was the few drops underneath the bottom of her head. Then, Mrs. Cunningham took off Sarah's bonnet. The underside was dripping wet with blood.

Dan Kelley took the bonnet along with some bloody rags the neighbors had used to wipe the back of Sarah's head and put them in the ash pile.

There was so much blood on the back of her head that the neighbors cut off some hair instead of trying to clean it. Effie Forbes saved the snipping of hair.

Effie and the others began to notice other details around the house. A dishpan full of bloody water at the end of the table in the kitchen that had been there since they arrived. A tin slop pail of bloody water in the storm shed. A hatchet that was lying on the floor close to where they first saw Sarah's body. Another hatchet by the coal box and a hairpin nearby.

And then there was that odd detail of a stick that had been propped underneath Sarah's chin to keep her mouth from opening. Strange, but…

It's hard to predict how people will act after a tragedy, especially when they're in a state of shock. Some people are highly emotional. Others are too stunned to react. Still others push aside their feelings to deal with the matters at hand. Keeping busy is a great distraction from feeling.

Death is hard and unpredictable. So is grief.

And homesteaders were nothing if not tough. They experienced physical hardships and life-threatening conditions every day just to survive and often were isolated far away from families and friends. If anybody could carry on through grief, a settler could.

But there was something about Dan Kelley that his neighbors were starting to wonder about.

Effie hadn't given it much thought when she first saw him walking slowly to the school to get help.

"I could not say he appeared to be excited," she said later.

Dan displayed the same demeanor at the house.

"He gave no signs of intense feelings," Effie said. "He appeared to be very collected."

H.J. Sinkie and W.A. Hoobler decided to go down into the cellar to have a look around. The cellar door was small: only about two feet by two feet or "wide enough for a good man to go through," as H.J. Sinkie described it. The cellar was described as being "as deep as a man is tall."

They lit a lantern, opened the trap door and descended down the steep ladder into the darkness of the cellar with a dirt floor and dirt walls. They saw the water tank where Dan said Sarah must have hit her head and a small pool of blood a couple feet away from it.

The two men said it looked as though the blood had dripped down into the basement, not as though she had fallen and bled in the cellar itself.

Chapter 6

John Kelley returned home from his business trip to Spring Lake to a scene that would haunt him for the rest of his life. He walked into his home that afternoon to see neighbors gathered and attending to the body of his mother.

The neighbors spent four days at the Kelley house. Dan would only be there for three of them.

Someone reported the suspicious circumstances to Buffalo County's sheriff and to the Justice of the Peace. A coroner's inquest was hastily called.

Officials secured the scene for their investigation, deputizing two people to guard the body of Sarah Kelley and two people to guard the premises.

They combed through the house and talked to the neighbors. Doctor Clara McManus and Doctor H.E. Jenkinson conducted a post-mortem examination at the house on Saturday, February 25, two days after Sarah died.

The exam and autopsy confirmed what the neighbors had seen as well as revealing more wounds that were even more severe.

The cuts on her forehead and on her head were up to two-and-one-half inches long. There was a deep cut in the back of her skull at the base of her brain. The doctor saw the imprints of fingerprint marks on both sides of Sarah's neck.

In addition, Dr. McManus observed one small fracture on her head and then a second larger fracture across her skull. She said the dura matar, the layer of tissue that covers the brain, was torn and Sarah's skull was split starting from the right side of the ear.

"The fracture ran clear over the coronal suture and was opened up," she said.[22]

Dr. McManus said the skull fractures alone would have been enough to cause death.

Sarah Kelley had no visible defensive wounds. Someone had attacked her, beaten her and choked her before she saw them or could defend herself or she was incapacitated before she could react.

The doctor's final assessment was somewhat of an understatement.

"I do not think it was from a fall," said Dr. McManus.

By Sunday, Dan Kelley was arrested on suspicion of murder and held in a cell in the Buffalo County Jail, all the while maintaining his innocence.

Chapter 7

Area newspapers reported the shocking news. In neighboring Hand County, this speculative headline ran in *The Pioneer Press*:

Murder or Suicide

Dan Kelly (sic) Charged With

Murder of His Wife[23]

The headline in *The Miller Sun* screamed:

Murder South of Us!

Daniel Kelly, (sic) In Buffalo

County Charged with

Killing his Wife

(Note: The name was spelled Kelly in several court documents.)

The Miller Sun reported a "theory" that Dan Kelley had hit his wife with a 2x4 board and threw her down into the cellar before bringing her back up, a theory that would be quickly questioned by someone who knew Dan.[24]

According to *The Miller Sun*, Dan telegraphed an attorney in Miller asking him to represent him.

But while he was sitting in the county jail, he had a visitor and a conversation that would make any defense attorney cringe.

W.J. Hughes was a business associate of the Kelleys and Dan was one of his best customers. He told the sheriff that he wanted to console Dan because "it was a hard case on the old man," who was almost 70.

The sheriff let him in and then stayed for part of the conversation.

Hughes asked Dan what had happened and questioned him, potentially giving him an out and then taking it away.

"Well, among other things, I told him that I thought that the old lady had fallen down the cellar was absolutely impossible."

He suggested that perhaps someone had slipped into the house while Dan was doing chores in the barn.

W.J. Hughes asked Dan, "Now, is it not possible that someone came along there and then he said, 'No sir. No one could come on the place without me seeing them.'"

Hughes threw out the possibility of temporary insanity or sudden passion.

"Then I said, 'Dan it's sufficient that someone killed her. I am going to ask you another question: Isn't it possible that as you been weak and sick that your mind was blank to a certain extent and committed the deed?'"

"He said 'No sir, my mind was as clear at that time as all times and it is at this time when I am talking to you.'"

Hughes continued, "I said it is very strange. I did not see how you got her up out of the cellar. You are feeble, old and not strong. How did you pull her out of the cellar? He said, 'I put my arms around her and walked off with her.'"

While Dan was sticking to his story, his visitor had just shot holes in it and raised more questions.

Hughes would later testify about the conversation at the trial in July. But it wouldn't be the most damaging testimony.

Chapter 8

On March 2, 1905, Gann Valley's hometown newspaper *The Dakota Chief* reported Sarah Kelley's death in a column about neighborhood happenings.

"It is the sad duty of the correspondent to note the death of Mrs. Daniel Kelly, who was reported at first to have met death by falling down cellar last Thursday morning, but later on the neighborhood was horrified with conflicting reports of a very serious nature of which the writer will leave for those who know to say. Mrs. Kelly was an old resident of Buffalo County and was well and favorably known by all the old settlers in Eden township where she lived. She was an ambitious and industrious woman, a good wife and a kind and loving mother. The writer well remembers her deep sorrow over the loss of a daughter who had passed away a few years before and she will ever be remembered as one of those quiet and unoffending persons who are much loved by the neighbors and friends."[25]

On that same day on a different page, the newspaper also carried another article reporting court news about the case. Dan Kelley appeared before a Justice of the Peace at a preliminary hearing to formally face charges one week after his wife was killed.

The people of Buffalo County packed into the courtroom to hear details of what had happened and to see the man accused of the crime.

The legal proceedings ran into the night and the next day.

The Dakota Chief's story said, "There was a large crowd of spectators present and much interest displayed in the progress of the case."[26]

As the newspaper pointed out, the Kelleys had been in Buffalo County for about twenty years and were known in the community. In a land where everybody had been newcomers within the past few decades, Dan and Sarah Kelley's arrival around 1887 made them essentially part of the establishment.

"Dan Kelly and his wife were among the old settlers of Buffalo County having lived as man and wife for about 40 years," the paper reported.[27]

But there would be no leniency for Dan as he waited for his trial. Justice of the Peace W.R. Eastman ordered Dan to be held without bail. He would be in jail until his trial date in the summer.

The Dakota Chief's headline and coverage of Dan's first court appearance read:

Held for Murder

Dan Kelly Charged with the

Horrible Crime of Wife Murder

In Jail Awaiting the June

Term of Court

The newspaper asked that members of the community keep their speculation to themselves so that an impartial jury could be chosen and the defendant could get a fair trial. The paper promised that it would do the same.

"It is only right and just to the community and all… …that we refrain from elaborating over the evidence or rumors or in commenting upon the case, however much our inclination as newspaper men might impel us to do so."

"We sincerely hope the guilt or innocence of the accused party will be established without passion or prejudice."[28]

Chapter 9

In July of 1905, as the Wright Brothers were revolutionizing transportation by developing their new flying machines and America was digging the Panama Canal, Gann Valley, South Dakota, was getting ready for its trial of the century.

In the months since his mother's murder and his father's arrest, 24-year-old John Kelley had had time to reflect on the tragedy.

Not only was his mother dead and his father facing the prospect of life in prison or the death penalty if he was convicted, there were concerns about the land the family had worked so hard to secure and develop. Then, there were the trial costs of paying the defense attorney.

As the surviving spouse, Dan Kelley sold one quarter of the land for $200 to his attorney John Pusey on March 1, 1905. Whether it was payment, collateral for payment or another reason is unclear. It's possible it was a way to eventually convey property that might be tangled up in court to Dan's son because John Kelley bought it from the attorney for the same price a month later in April.

To make matters even worse, John Kelley was subpoenaed to testify by the prosecution team.

On July 18, 1905, the folks of Buffalo County gathered at 10 o'clock in the morning at the courthouse for the trial. Fifty potential jurors were subpoenaed and then whittled down to 12 jury members with one alternate juror.

"It was nearly supper time when the jury was impaneled," *The Dakota Chief* reported.[29]

The all-male jury included names Dan knew: Thomas Chopkie, Alex Gilchrist, Jesse Costello, A.W. Miller, Henry Sculte, Oscar Dearborn, Chris Andison, Albert Harwig, Nels Krog, John Henrichsen and Henry Klindt, whose son August Klindt would become the sheriff of Buffalo County in the 1940's and, at 7'2" inches tall, would become known as the Gann Valley giant. The jury also included Ed Etbauer, whose great grandson Billy Etbauer would become a world champion bronc rider on the rodeo circuit in the 1990's and 2000's.

The prosecutors were Virginia born and Indiana raised James Cook, who was a civil war veteran and served as the Buffalo County State's Attorney. His co-counsel James Brown from the larger town of Chamberlain, would later serve as an assistant attorney general in South Dakota and on the state Supreme Court.

The trial ran into the night as the prosecutors began presenting their case. Neighbors, including H.J. Sinkie, and schoolteacher Effie Forbes testified about what they saw at the house. The doctors who performed the postmortem examination of Sarah Kelley testified about the wounds they saw on her body.

But the prosecution's star witness would be pivotal in the case. The prosecutors had found a motive and they needed Dan Kelley's son John to talk about it.

While the Kelleys had appeared to be faring well during the drought years when some of the other farmers were facing foreclosure, Dan Kelley, in fact, had also accumulated debt. He had taken out a loan when he bought the additional quarter of land at a foreclosure sale in 1896.

With drought withering his profits and facing the possibility that he too could lose his land, Dan came up with a plan. Even though women still didn't have the right to vote in federal elections, they were allowed to own land.

The Homestead Act of 1862 allowed single, widowed and divorced women to claim 160 acres of land, but a married woman still was not allowed to claim land unless she was considered the head of the household.[30]

However, when South Dakota gained statehood in 1889, the new state constitution granted women the right to own separate property and they would not be liable for their husband's debts.[31]

It was the perfect timing for the perfect solution.

Dan decided to put 160 acres of land in his wife's name and deeded it over to her. He also put his cattle and horses in her name.

No land. No collateral. No chance of foreclosure.

It gave him time to work through the bad financial times. And it worked.

The good times returned and the crops and the money were coming in again. The town of Gann Valley was booming with stores and banks opening.

So Dan asked Sarah to deed the land back to him. There was a problem, though.

And that was the focus of the state's questioning of John Kelley on the witness stand.

John was living with his parents in their house, which meant he saw their interactions every day. And Prosecutor James Cook wanted the jury to hear about it.

John Kelley took the stand, a son in the terrible position of testifying against his father in the murder of his mother. The prosecutor took little time getting to the point.

Prosecutor Cook: "State whether your father or mother had quarrels?"[32]

John Kelley: "Yes, sir. They had some quarrels."

Prosecutor Cook: "What were the quarrels about?"

The defense attorney objected to the question at this point. The objection was overruled by the judge and the prosecution's line of questioning continued.

Prosecutor Cook: "What were the quarrels about if for any particular reason?"

John Kelley: "Sometimes there was a quarrel about the property."

Prosecutor Cook: "About the property where you live?"

John Kelley: "Yes, sir."

Prosecutor Cook: "What was it your father wanted done about the property?"

John Kelley: "Well, most of the property had been deeded to mother."

Prosecutor Cook: "What did he want?"

John Kelley: "He wanted it back again."

Prosecutor Cook: "Had it been done?"

John Kelley: "It had not."

Prosecutor Cook: "State whether your mother refused to deed it back."

John Kelley: "She refused."

    Damaging, yes. But there was more damage to come. And it came from Dan's own attorney as he cross examined his client's son.

Chapter 10

Dan Kelley's defense attorney, a state legislator, also served as the state's attorney in neighboring Hand County. The county prosecutor. And John Pusey had the doggedness of prosecutorial zeal. His cross examination of Dan's son was far longer than that of the Buffalo County prosecutors. And far more destructive to his client's claim of innocence.

John Pusey had objected to the line of questioning about the land and the subsequent questions about the Kelley's arguments. But, since the subject was out there, the prosecutor-turned-defense-attorney had to address it.

Maybe he could convince the jurors that Dan wasn't the instigator of the arguments. Maybe John didn't really know the whole story if he wasn't there all the time.

Maybe he could show that someone else had a motive. Maybe John had an unrevealed financial stake or a financial motive himself. Maybe he could poke some holes in John's testimony or make the jury wonder if it was the son who had injured his mother.

It takes reasonable doubt for a jury to vote not guilty in a trial. It doesn't take overwhelming doubt.

Defense Attorney Pusey: "Had you heard them quarrel yourself?"

John Kelley: "Yes sir."

Defense Attorney Pusey: "How… did your father and mother quarrel about this property very often?"

John Kelley: "Well, I could not say yes. They quarreled quite frequently and I could not say how often."

Defense Attorney Pusey: "You have been living at home right along for the last three years."

John Kelley: "Yes sir. That has been my home where I growed up."

Defense Attorney Pusey: "Have you been at home yourself the last three years?"

John Kelley: "Yes sir."

Defense Attorney Pusey: "All the time?"

John Kelley: "Any more than I was out working out some place, like last summer, I was out boring wells. I would not be home all the time and always been back and forth sometime."

Defense Attorney Pusey: "How long have you been in the well boring business?"

John Kelley: "Well, I could not just say. I should judge about four or five years. I did not hardly know the business for some time. Maybe there would be six months I would not move or touch it."

Defense Attorney Pusey: "Then you would be out again boring wells?"

John Kelley: "Well, last summer I was out one time and hardly began until they began with harvest."

With John living at home, but away from home on business sometimes established, Pusey moved on to the subject of the arguments.

Defense Attorney Pusey: "When these quarrels were, John, did you take any part in them yourself?"

John Kelley: "I would not take any part in them, but if they got together, I had to get between them."

Defense Attorney Pusey: "When the trouble would get to be of such a nature, sometimes that they would meet in a personal encounter?"

John Kelley: "Yes, sir."

Defense Attorney Pusey: "Which one of the two would be the originator of the trouble? If either, which would commence? In regard to farm, land and the cattle, was it your father?"

John Kelley: "Yes, sir."

Dan Kelley's defense attorney zeroed in on the issue of the livestock. Everybody, it appeared, had a stake in something at the Kelley homestead.

Defense Attorney Pusey: "Well, now, it is true that your father, your mother and you all claimed some property?"

John Kelley: "Yes, sir."

Defense Attorney Pusey: "You had some horses there?"

John Kelley: "Yes, sir."

Defense Attorney Pusey: "How many head did you have?"

The prosecution objected to this question. The judge ruled for the prosecution and John Pusey dropped the question about the number of horses John housed at his parent's farm. Then he focused on trying to make the livestock a general source of contention all around.

Defense Attorney Pusey: "Now, was there any quarrels between you and your father and your mother in regard to the horses you claimed there?"

John Kelley: "There was not."

Defense Attorney Pusey: "Well, was there any quarreling any of the.... You just state what the quarrels was about: what particular property or horses and cattle was the quarrel about, or whether it was cattle or not. Was it cattle they quarreled about?"

John Kelley: "They quarreled about the cattle."

Defense Attorney Pusey: "And what seemed to be the nature of their quarrel: what did each one want?"

John Kelley: "The nature of the quarrel seemed to be that he wanted to deed them back."

Defense Attorney Pusey: "Well, why did he say he wanted them back?"

John Kelley: "Well, it would be like any... they wanted to get them back again what was deed to them in the first place."

With the contentious nature of the conflict over the land and livestock, the defense attorney appeared to be trying to establish that everybody had a vested interest in the chattel and the cattle. The defense attorney also tried to suggest that maybe the arguments weren't always one-sided in terms of who started them.

Defense Attorney Pusey: "You say they quarreled about other business?"

John Kelley: "They would quarrel about other little matters."

Defense Attorney Pusey: "Who generally started these quarrels?"

John Kelley: "Well, to the best of my knowledge, it would be my father."

Defense Attorney Pusey: "You think he generally started them?"

John Kelley: "Yes, sir."

Defense Attorney Pusey: "What would you say about your father's or mother's temper?"

John Kelley: "They had a high temper."

Defense Attorney Pusey: "Both of them?"

John Kelley: "Yes, sir."

Defense Attorney Pusey: "It would not take much to start to fuss and quarrel if either wanted it?"

John Kelley: "No."

Defense Attorney Pusey: "You say both were ready for racket or trouble any time, would you?"

John Kelley: "She did not just want to quarrel until something started it."

By this time, the jury had learned that the land had been in Sarah Kelley's name for about nine years.

In his next question, the defense attorney implied that perhaps Sarah Kelley should have been more appreciative of the transfer of land, suggesting that maybe she should have shown more gratitude. A classic strategy of blaming the victim.

A little patriarchal, perhaps, but it just might work in a culture where women still had a lower status in society despite their new status as land-owners and where everyone in the county had earned their land with hard labor, sweat and sheer survival skills.

A man's home is his castle no matter if it's a rickety claim shanty, a sod house or a sturdy, well-built wood house. John Pusey was about to appeal to their enormous pride of ownership and maybe to some old-fashioned patriarchal pride.

He reminded the jury that Sarah had the land in her name because of her husband.

Defense Attorney Pusey: "Now, John, before this land was deeded to your mother, were the cattle… that is gifted to her the same time?"

John Kelley: "Yes, sir."

Under further defense questioning, the jury heard that life had not always been contentious in the Kelley household. The transferred deed had changed the family dynamics.

Defense Attorney Pusey: "Before that deed, did they have any quarrels?"

John Kelley: "I do not remember they had. The first quarrel then, is when they had this quarrel over the property."

The disagreements began to escalate two or three years before the murder. John testified that he was out working on the farm one day and walked back into the house to find that a fight had turned physical. His father had hit his mother.

But she still didn't relent on the land. So, after one fight, Dan Kelley walked out.

Defense Attorney Pusey: "Did your mother order him to leave her that time?"

John Kelley: "No, she did not."

Defense Attorney Pusey: "Where did he go when he left."

John Kelley: "He went to Will Morrow's."

Defense Attorney Pusey: "How long did he remain away from home that time?"

John Kelley: "Two weeks."

Defense Attorney Pusey: "How did he happen to come back?"

John Kelley: "He just came back."

Defense Attorney Pusey: "Did your mother send for him to come back?"

John Kelley: "I don't think so. Not that I know of."

Defense Attorney Pusey: "Did you send for him to come back?"

John Kelley: "I did not."

The defense attorney's long line of questioning about the fights opened a floodgate for the prosecution. There was more to the fight that John had walked in on. John testified that his father had struck Sarah when his sister Maime was still living at home as a second witness.

The prosecution team pounced on it. They only had four questions during their re-direct examination of John Kelley.

Prosecutor James Brown asked if Dan Kelley had used more "blows or violence" during the fight.

John Kelley: "Well, he was going to hit her with a chair."

Prosecutor Brown: "Did you interfere?"

John Kelley: "Yes, I did. When I came in my father was in the front room and she…. The chair struck the door. He broke the (door) panels when I came in."

Chapter 11

There's an old saying that when you find yourself digging your own hole, maybe you should put down the shovel and stop digging.

After the defense attorney's own questions established that Dan Kelley had started the fights and that he had hit Sarah, defense attorney John Pusey appeared to move on to another premise.

Just because someone has used violence in the past, doesn't mean they're capable of killing someone. People can get mad and still know when to stop. After all, Dan did leave home after a big fight to cool off.

The defense established that after the fight in July 1904, the situation seemed to de-escalate.

The only disagreement John Kelley observed that fall and during the winter of 1904 and 1905 was a minor squabble about a matter unrelated to the property just a few weeks before Sarah was killed, begging the question: had Dan Kelley accepted his fate as a farmer, husband and partner, but not as an owner of the property?

John Pusey asked John Kelley if his parents had had a disagreement the night before Sarah died. No, they hadn't.

On the morning of February 23, John was eating breakfast while his father was getting up. Nothing appeared to be amiss.

Since Maime had moved out of the house to work for someone the previous Fall, Pusey established that the only people there on February 23 were Dan and Sarah Kelley, John Kelley and John Hanson, John's business partner in his well-drilling business.

"This man, Hanson," as the defense attorney referred to him.

The defense could use the de-escalation of the arguments to suggest that Dan had decided to live with his status as a non-land owner, mitigating his motive and leaving open the possibility that it could mean that someone else might have committed the crime.

The prosecution could use the same information to persuade the jury that Dan stopped arguing because he had decided what he was going to do.

Chapter 12

The prosecutors wrapped up their witness testimony and rested their case by noon of the second day of the trial.

That afternoon, the defense case began with its own star witness.

Dan Kelley himself took the stand. It was his last chance to give his account of what happened and try to save himself from life in prison or from hanging from the gallows.

His trial testimony was lost from county court records over the years, but Gann Valley's *Dakota Chief* described the scene and Dan's court appearance this way:

"The defendant was put on the stand immediately after dinner and the courtroom was crowded to hear the story from the lips of the accused man."

"He presented a tragic appearance, an old man of nearly 70 years of age with hair and whiskers as white as snow on the witness stand with the murder of his wife and upon his testimony depended on large extent the escape of the prisoner from a prison sentence or death on the gallows."[33]

Effie Forbes had described Dan as calm and unemotional after Sarah was killed and he held his composure on the stand as well.

His testimony, in which he appears to have stuck to the same story he told his neighbors, was riveting to courtroom observers.

The Dakota Chief reported, "His story was dramatic in the extreme and his calm demeanor as he told his story drawn out by his attorney John Pusey and ready answers to rigid cross examination conducted by James Brown was remarkable and but for a few damaging admissions created a sentiment in his favor."[34]

After Dan's testimony, several neighbors were called to the witness stand to testify about Dan Kelley's "former good character," as *The Dakota Chief* reported.

Testimony concluded by 4:30 that afternoon and closing arguments began with a short statement by Prosecutor James Cook.

It appears the closing procedures were typical of modern trials where the prosecution team often breaks down their closing statements into two parts beginning with a short statement about the charges and procedural aspects of the case. Then, the defense makes its closing argument before the second prosecutor speaks, laying out the facts and laying bare the emotion of the case on behalf of the victim and the state.

If defense attorney John Pusey had hit some shaky territory in his cross-examination of his client's son, he appears to have impressed courtroom spectators with his closing statement.

The Dakota Chief reported: "John Pusey "made a long and forcible plea for his client."[35]

The defense attorney's final plea for his client's freedom and his life wrapped up about 11 o'clock that night.

The next morning, Prosecutor John Brown presented a two-hour long closing argument to the jury, ending before noon.

The jury was well into their deliberations by the afternoon. By 4 p.m., Jury Foreman Oscar Dearborn announced the jury's verdict. The 12 members of the jury agreed with the state's charges that Dan Kelley had:

"with force and arms, willfully, unlawfully, feloniously, with malice aforethought, and with a premeditated design to effect the death of Sarah Kelly, a human being, did then and there make an assault upon said Sarah Kelly, and did choke and beat her to death and the said Daniel Kelly with a certain deadly weapon… …did then and there, willfully, unlawfully, feloniously, with malice aforethought, and with premediated design to effect the death of said Sarah Kelly, strike, beat and wound the said Sarah Kelly upon her head, thereby inflicting upon her several mortal wounds, of which mortal wounds the said Sarah Kelly."

On July 20, 1905, Dan Kelley was convicted of premeditated murder and sentenced to life imprisonment in the state penitentiary. He had escaped the death sentence of hanging from the gallows, but he would never be a free man again.

Dan had remained stoic since his arrest and throughout the trial testimony, but *The Dakota Chief* reported that hearing his guilty verdict and his life sentence was more than Dan could bear. He broke down.[36]

The Dakota Chief hammered out the story for its deadline that night.

But it was not front page news, possibly because time constraints of the old-fashioned method of writing on typewriters, and then physically type-setting the story onto paper meant that the story had to be dropped into whatever space was available for it without re-arranging the whole paper. Regardless, the story made the paper for citizens to read the next day.

The story of the verdict also ran on the inside pages of Miller's *Pioneer Press* with a one-line headline.

A Life Sentence

The newspaper account read: "Daniel Kelly, of Buffalo County, was found guilty of murdering his aged wife, in the circuit court last week at Gannvalley (sic) and was sentenced to imprisonment for life."

The *Pioneer Press* article also contained this line:

"In an interview with the reporter, Attorney Pusey states that there was not much to hang a defense on as the old man was alone with his wife and was unable to corroborate his own story."[37]

The verdict was big news all over the state. In South Dakota's largest city of Sioux Falls, *The Argus Leader's* headline read:

Evidence of Brutal Crime

Testimony Brought out Startling Facts

Pleases Buffalo County

General Sentiment is that Old

Man Deserves his Life

Sentence

The Argus Leader said the case "was probably the hardest fought battle ever waged in the courts of this part of the state. The defendant made a strong witness for himself and stoutly maintained his story against a strong fire of cross-examination, and but for some very damaging admissions at times created some sentiment in his favor."

But the article pointed out, "The state brought out a long chain of circumstantial evidence in substantiation of their belief that Kelley was the slayer of his wife."

Dan's countenance again came under scrutiny. *The Argus Leader* reported, "The defendant maintained a stolid indifference until he received his sentence but broke down upon arriving at the jail when he was placed in his cell."

The story concluded with this assessment: "The general sentiment is that the jury brought in a just verdict."[38]

Dan Kelley spent the rest of his life locked up in South Dakota's state penitentiary in Sioux Falls.

He died there of apoplexy on July 21, 1911, six years after Sarah was murdered and exactly six years to the day that he entered prison.

A notice in *The Pioneer Press* announced his death and said the prison system had contacted the family and was holding his remains subject to their orders. The article said: "Notwithstanding that he was a lifer, he has been a model prisoner."[39]

There's no indication that the family claimed his body for burial.

Sarah Kelley was buried a few miles from her home, where she would rest quietly for more than one hundred years before she became the center of attention again.

Part 2

Life After The Trial

Chapter 13

For several years, John Kelley lived on the farm where his father had killed his mother.

When his mother's estate was settled in 1909, he bought his two siblings' shares of their inherited land.

But, ten years later as the Spanish flu epidemic raged, John sold the homestead and left his life in Buffalo County behind. He moved to neighboring Hand County.

About a year after that, the blue-eyed bachelor married Anna Steinleitner. Anna had a calm and soothing personality, so she was exactly what a man who had been traumatized by family tragedy needed.

She had borne four daughters with her first husband, who died from the Spanish flu. John and Anna had four more daughters together.

Now, John Kelley was dad to eight girls. In the 1940's, when John was about 60, he would raise two more girls after two of Anna's daughters died within a short time of each another, one within two weeks after childbirth.

Joan Joy was almost three years old when her mother Cleone, who was Anna's daughter from her first marriage, died in a fire in 1943. Cleone was starting the coal-fueled cookstove in their farmhouse when she poured kerosene over the coals to light them. A fire erupted that burned her so badly that she succumbed to her injuries.

So, little Joan went to live with her grandparents on their farm. She called Anna "Mom" and she called her step-grandfather "Grandpa."

Joan's memories are of a happy home. Two of her aunts were still living in the house with their parents and they fussed over the two little girls, holding tea parties with them. Anna liked to fish and often took the children and grandchildren with her.

Joan remembers that John was tall, but isn't sure if he was so tall or if he just appeared tall to a little girl. He clearly remembers that he was slender and industrious.

"He sure was a hard worker," she said.

He was also very quiet.

Whether he was always quiet or became more taciturn after his mother was killed isn't known. But a murder in the family isn't something that easily lends itself to casual conversation or to conversations that fall upon the ears of toddlers.

Joan overheard whispers about John's mother when the adults apparently thought she was too young to understand what they were talking about.

But the child eventually caught on to the fact that something had happened.

"I knew that she had been killed," Joan said. "I knew her husband did it."

When Joan was old enough to comprehend more about the conversations going on around her, the whispered words among the adults stopped.

She never heard anything about the case from John Kelley.

"He never talked about it," said Joan.

John Kelley had talked about it enough. He had to testify in the coroner's inquest. Then he had to testify at the trial.

John, it appeared, wanted to forget. For awhile, he tried to numb his painful memories with alcohol.

"I had heard that John was quite a drinker in his younger years," Joan said.

But that changed with Anna's soothing demeanor and the laughter of children. Joan never saw any alcohol in the house and John seldom went to town.

Joan never heard if John had ever contacted or visited his father at the state penitentiary or if he had completely cut ties.

And while it appears that there was no response to the prison's public newspaper announcement of Dan's death, John's new family didn't know if he had buried his father or if he had just let the prison system bury him as it does when no one claims an inmate's remains.

Sarah's grave was a mystery as well.

Part 3

A Century Later

Chapter 14

Sarah Kelley was buried in a picturesque and bucolic cemetery on a windswept hill less than five miles from her home in Buffalo County.

In the summertime, butterflies flit through the air and birds trill, sharing their songs from the leafy branches of the cedar tree in the middle of the church yard. Evergreen trees line the north side of the cemetery.

A peaceful place. A gentle sigh of relief.

During holiday ceremonies and burial services, cows in the neighboring pasture often walk up to the fence and watch the activities, staring in wide-eyed silence at the people gathered there.

In the days before automobiles, Sarah Kelley would have been carried in a wagon or hearse pulled by horses over the sloping hills leading to the small graveyard that lies in the presence of pastures and deep in the heart of the community.

Saint Placidus Duncan Church is the essence of community. The parish was formed in 1887 and the first church structure was built around 1889.

Like the people who settled this raw land, the church itself is a symbol of resilience. The original church was destroyed by a tornado in 1924 when the winds picked it up and turned it around on its foundation to face east instead of south.

The congregation built a bigger church to replace it in 1925. Just a year later, lightning struck and started a fire that destroyed the new church.

Undaunted, parishioners built yet another one. A fire started near the altar of that church on Easter Sunday in 1929, but the fire somehow self-extinguished before it caused significant damage. Church members called it a miracle.[40]

The third chapel, a registered historic landmark, stands as an architectural model of what you imagine when you think of a country church: white clapboard with a gable roof and a classic steeple on the top. The gothic shaped windows are partially covered with gauze curtains in the tradition of the original church. A small old-fashioned organ sits on a balcony above the pews.

Generations of families have been buried in this cemetery and their descendants make sure their ancestors are not forgotten. This is a community that reveres its dead. The congregation sees that the church is neatly kept and the grounds and the graves are neatly manicured.

There were only about half a dozen graves in the cemetery when Sarah Kelley was placed in the loamy soil not long after the turn of the 20th century.

But, interestingly, her grave was placed a noticeable distance away from the other graves, so far that it appeared isolated. And very lonely.

The reason was lost to time.

Over the years, the details of what happened to her were also forgotten by many folks around Buffalo County.

People in the Gann Valley area didn't talk much about the case as the trial became more distant in the past so future generations heard only snippets of the story if they heard anything at all.

As years slipped into decades, no family members came to visit the grave of Sarah Kelley. No relatives left flowers. No one came to grieve for this pioneer woman who lost her life over the very thing that had brought all their ancestors to the new Dakota Territory that became South Dakota.

Sarah's grave would have been lonely indeed if not for the faithful of Duncan Church.

Church members maintain the cemetery year-round, but they go all-out for Memorial Day, when the old soldiers of Buffalo County come to play taps, hoist the flag and fire a 21-gun salute for the war veterans who are buried here.

Members of the congregation place flags and flowers at the gravesites of all the veterans. And they place bouquets on every grave so that everyone is remembered even if their families are long gone from here.

Every year, as they distribute the flowers to the gravesites, they place flowers on Sarah Kelley's grave too. So, while Sarah Kelley's grave looked all alone in the far corner of the cemetery, it was not lonely in the sense that she has people she doesn't even know who look after her in her final resting place.

But they often wondered. And they speculated. Why was this woman buried in a grave that was so far away from the others?

Was she a victim of one of the deadly diphtheria or typhoid epidemics that swept through the Great Plains? Epidemic victims were often buried far away from others in cemeteries because people in the early 1900's were concerned that the germs might still be viable around the gravesites.

Was she a notorious outlaw who was separated from the others because she brought shame to her family or to the community?

Was she someone who was just passing through, died along the way and was buried at the nearest church?

The way to the West was lined with unknown, unmarked graves. If someone died along the way on a wagon train, there was seldom a town in the vast expanse of prairie and certainly no cemetery, so settlers often buried their dead near their campsite. Then, they had to move on to their destination and were forced to leave their loved ones behind.

So, maybe she was buried in the distant grave just because she was not a church member, but was allowed to be buried in the cemetery anyway.

Robert Scholten, one of the church members who dutifully maintained the cemetery and mowed the grass around the graves for years, says the explanation that most people began to settle upon was that she must have met her demise by her own hand.

"At Duncan, it was just widely accepted and said that she had committed suicide and that's why she was over there in that corner," Scholten said.

In 1905, the Catholic Church did not allow suicide victims to be buried in Catholic cemeteries.

But, when it comes to the delicate matters of life and death and grief, there are no strangers in a strange land. Settlers who had all moved far from their original homes surely could have made an exception out of compassion.

Speculation aside, Sarah Kelley still had no family who visited. No church member living in the mid to late 20th or early 21st century ever saw any relatives at the cemetery nor saw any flowers on her grave except for the church flowers.

The grave would have been hard to find anyway. The tombstone not only stands in the far corner of the graveyard by the adjoining farmland, but it's partially hidden by the evergreen trees that were planted after she was buried. You'd barely notice the grave at all if you didn't know it was there.

Sarah Kelley's headstone is an indication that her family cared enough to purchase a sizeable tombstone. A relic of a bygone era, it's shaped like a stacked, squared off obelisk with a topper in the style that was popular at the time.

The stone shows crumbles of age now. The decorative topper fell off at one point, so church members bought a new granite ball and paid to have it placed on top. Just another gesture to show respect to those who came before us.

The etching on Sarah's name on the stone has softened over the years and you have to look closely to see it even if it hadn't been pointing inward toward the evergreens. For years, the only way to see the name was to step into the branches on the other side to look at it.

One family member apparently did try to find it. Richard Sinkie was having lunch at a café in Miller one day when a woman approached him. She'd been asking around and someone had told her the Sinkie family bought the Kelley land in 1919. Her family's land.

She told him she was from California and was wondering if he knew where the woman who was murdered on the land was buried. Maybe on the land itself?

No, Richard told her, the grave was not on the land.

He didn't know that Sarah was buried just five miles from the old homestead. He was not a member of Duncan Church and the location of the church and cemetery is not one you go to unless you have a specific reason.

After the woman left, Richard's wife Karen Sinkie went to collect payment for usage of a hunting lodge that Robert Scholten had rented for some family members. She told him about the murder and the mystery of where the victim's grave was located.

Robert asked who the murder victim was and was surprised to hear that it was a grave he knew well: the lonely grave that he and the other church members cared for at St. Placidus Duncan Cemetery.

He would later take the information about the murder of Sarah Kelley to the other members of the congregation.

"To me, that was the day that history got changed at Duncan Church because then we knew that it wasn't suicide. We knew that it was a murder," Robert Scholten said. "Now we know what the truth is."

Church members don't know if the woman, who they presumed to be a descendant of Charles Kelley who had moved to California, ever made her way to Duncan cemetery to find Sarah's grave. But, to a certain extent, it was enough to know that someone had tried. It also established that she had relatives out there somewhere.

The information that Sarah Kelley had been killed came just in time to get it into a booklet they were working on for the church's 125th anniversary celebration.

As church members pored through old church documents for information about historical events and the names of everyone buried there, church member Kathy Yost went to the courthouse to look up more information about the case so she could include it with the church history in the anniversary booklet.

Now, Duncan Church had some answers about what had happened to Sarah Kelley, but still no answers as to why she was buried so far away from the others.

The mystery of her placement may never be solved. But the questions about what happened to her family would be answered nine years later.

Chapter 15

One day in the Fall of 2021, after years of never seeing any signs of visitation, Kathy Yost arrived at the cemetery to see flowers on Sarah Kelley's grave.

Someone had finally found the grave of their pioneer ancestor who had been so brutally murdered.

The missing link was provided by an article published in *South Dakota Magazine*, written by the author of this book.

It told the story of the homicide, the motive, one family member's attempt to find the grave decades ago, and modern church members' tender attention to the graves. It reached the eyes of descendants of Sarah and Dan Kelley and finally gave them answers about what had happened in their family's past.

Annette Alumbaugh, Sarah Kelley's great granddaughter, was getting ready to play cards with friends when she got a phone call from her friend Jane Krebs.

"Jane Krebs called me and said, 'You're not going to believe what was in the *South Dakota Magazine*!'"

Annette's mother Lucille was Sarah and John Kelley's daughter. Lucille had never talked about the family tragedy and Annette was 30 or 35-years-old before she ever heard anything about it at all. She was at a restaurant having dinner with her mother and her Aunt Doris Biddle in Sioux Falls when Doris suddenly said, "Hey, do you know about your great grandpa?"

Aunt Doris only knew that Dan Kelley had killed Sarah, but didn't know the details. Annette's mother remained silent throughout the conversation and Annette didn't invade her mom's silent space to ask more questions later.

Annette's neighbor worked in the parole division of the state prison system so she asked him if he could find any information about Dan Kelley.

The only information he found was that Dan apparently wasn't happy to be in prison and had died there in 1911 of apoplexy, likely of a brain hemorrhage.

At the time that Annette asked her neighbor for information about Dan, she didn't think about asking where he had been buried.

But now, after seeing the *South Dakota Magazine* article, she finally knew what had happened to Sarah and where she was buried.

Annette's daughter Jill Wallace immediately took flowers to the grave and then called Kathy Yost, who was quoted in the magazine article.

Later, Jill would have Sarah's tombstone turned around so the name faces outward instead of facing in toward the trees where the name is not visible.

Family members had already started trying to learn about their family history through genealogy work. Eileen Wilson, whose husband Tom was John and Anna's grandson, was tracing their family tree through census records and obituaries. They found that Dan and Sarah lived in Ireland and Scotland before immigrating to the United States when John was about two years old.

And now that they knew that someone from California had looked for Sarah's grave years ago, they intensified the search for members of Charles Kelley's family there.

They compared notes with Kathy Yost, who had done more research herself after she first found information about the case during the church's 125th anniversary celebration. Eileen was happy for the help and information when she and Tom finally met her.

"We all went and we just ate up everything she had to give up," said Eileen.

Members of Duncan Church were glad that most of the mystery was solved, that the family had some answers and closure, and that they had played a central role in it.

Church members discussed the case and the journey to find family with their priest. And they had an idea.

They didn't know if Sarah had had a funeral in 1905. Maybe she did. She had a nice headstone after all. But maybe there was too much trauma, too much confusion and just too much pain and sadness to hold a formal ceremony at the time.

There was no record of her funeral in the church log books, but it's possible that it just wasn't recorded or it wasn't recorded because the wake and funeral were held at her home. They just didn't know. But they were determined that Sarah would have some kind of formal remembrance at the church now that family had been found and wanted to visit the grave.

They asked Father Kevin Doyle if they could dedicate a service honoring Sarah Kelley even though she had died 117 years ago.

The priest agreed. "I said, let's do it because we can always have the option of a mass for the dead."

On a sunny Tuesday afternoon in July 2022, they gathered under the steeply pitched ceiling of Duncan Church, sitting on the wooden pews facing the little blue alcove that houses the altar that still has some burn marks on it from the 1929 Easter Day fire.

About a dozen of Sarah Kelley's relatives were there.

Richard Sinkie, who was living on the land that had been the Kelley's homestead, was in attendance with members of his family.

Community members who weren't members of Duncan Church also showed up just like their ancestors had shown up to stand up for Sarah Kelley and testify at the coroner's inquest and at the trial.

All were solemn, respectful and a little curious to hear what the priest would say about Sarah Kelley and this dark part of the history of Buffalo County.

Father Doyle didn't focus on the brutal way that Sarah was killed when he spoke to the congregation.

"I said, "Everybody already knows the story and they all kind of nodded their heads. We don't need to go there."

Father Doyle talked about finding light out of the darkness.

"Something tragic did occur and even though it was 100 years ago, it's still something that we want to say to the family that even out of the worst circumstances good can come from it."

"Let's give Sarah as much honor as we possibly can and so anything that was lacking at the time we're gonna make up for right now. We're gonna give Sarah everything that we can possibly give her from this world for her sake."

Himself a descendant of homesteading immigrants on his mother's side, Father Doyle still has a letter that his great grandfather wrote proudly telling his family back home that he and his family had arrived safely in Dakota Territory and now owned land that would have been forever out of their reach in their native Ireland.

He talked about the hardships that all of their ancestors had endured in the old West to help put their children and grandchildren where they are today.

"Everybody thinks it's like a Louis L'Amour story, but it's a lot of work. It's a lot of sacrifice and people having to work with each other and depression setting in and all that kind of stuff."

"We want to honor those who truly were the victims of the sacrifices that we just take for granted in the 21st century."

The walls of the tiny church reverberated with prayers and the songs "Gather Us In," "Softly and Tenderly Jesus is Calling Me Home" and "How Great Thou Art," accompanied by the strumming of Allan Knippling's wooden guitar.

After the service, attendees walked out into the cemetery for a graveside ceremony just as they would for any other funeral. They clustered around the grave that sat by itself among the evergreens as Father Doyle recited prayers and they all sang "Song of Farewell."

The family placed more flowers on the grave: red and white petunias, and mixed flowers of orange, yellow and lavender in a tree trunk container, rustic yet elaborate as though they were making up for the lost years.

Then, everyone walked up the wooden steps back into the church and gathered together for a potluck dinner with home cooked dishes and the camaraderie that is an integral part of funerals and special services at the church.

They traded stories of their own homesteader ancestors and remembered all the work that went into the land where they carry on the family tradition of farming and ranching.

They talked about Sarah Kelley and expressed belated condolences to her descendants.

After the service, Richard Sinkie invited the family to come to his farm, the former Kelley homestead, to see where their ancestors had lived. He let them take stones from the old foundation as a remembrance, parts of their past that had been lost and then found again.

After everything that had happened in the past and all that had been lost with time, it was comforting to hold a tangible piece of their ancestors' lives.

"Daniel and Sarah, I would assume, built the buildings themselves. Back then, they had to have done most of the work themselves so it's just a family connection," said Annette.

It had come full circle.

The folks of Buffalo County had come together again to stand up for a crime victim who had touched the community's heart in the cold winter of 1905 and still does more than a century later.

On this warm summer day more than 100 years later, Sarah Kelley had family again and she had friends she didn't even know in a tiny country church with an enormous heart.

Friends who look after her grave.

Friends who remember her.

Friends and family who bring her flowers.

Part 4

Living with

The Past

Chapter 16

When Lee Sinkie took over the farm from his father Richard, he became the fifth generation in his family to farm in Buffalo County and a custodian of the land with the tragic past.

"My uncle would refer to that pasture as the Kelley quarter," Lee recalled.

After the Sinkies bought the Kelley homestead in 1919, they never lived in the Kelley house and eventually tore it down.

Around the 1950's or early 1960's, Richard's father sold the rocks that were the base of the house foundation to the U.S. Army Corps of Engineers for fifty cents a ton. The Army Corps used them to build the Big Bend Dam, which is located on the Missouri River at the western edge of Buffalo County.

Today, only a few scattered stones mark the spot where the Kelley house once stood, a sad testament to all that is left of their shattered American dream.

"All the things they went through to get here and then to have it come to that. It falls apart like that," Lee Sinkie laments.

Like his dad, Lee is mindful of what happened here and respectful of it.

While his father often thought about Sarah Kelley when he was mowing the pasture for hay, Lee sometimes thinks about what happened to her too.

"If I'm out fixing fence, you pause to think."

He sees the site as part of history and as a reminder of the people who came before him, of the homesteaders who faced obstacles he can only imagine.

When the Sinkie family arrived in Buffalo County around 1883, the tall grass hid the heavy rocks on the ground, stones that had to removed by hand before the settlers could even begin to steer a single blade plow that was pulled by horse or oxen to break the ten untouched acres of tough sod as required under the Homestead Act.

"I can't imagine being the first person to put a plow into that land," said Deb Morrison.

In addition to the scattered rocks from the foundation, there is still an impression in the ground from the house and where the Kelleys dug a storm cellar.

Lee tries to visualize what it was like in the homestead days: where the buildings stood and where the road or path into the homestead was located.

"It's intriguing to me at certain times of the year when the vegetation is down."

And occasionally Lee and Deb find a remnant of something from the past poking through the dirt, bits and pieces of life that went on here before them.

"We find the coolest things and we wonder who put it there," said Deb.

One time, they found a weathered, galvanized tub. They're not sure if it's from Sarah Kelley's days there, John's after she died, or if it was used in later years by someone else working on the land.

But the items are artifacts of sorts and they treat them as such. With respect. They don't remove them. They stay with the land.

"We put them back."

Part 5

Historical Perspective

Psychological Challenges of Homesteading

Chapter 17

The Homestead Act required settlers to work their land for five years to prove up their claim before they could earn legal title to the homestead.

It could be a long five years and a torrid test of their very survival skills.

Richard Edwards, the director emeritus for the Center for Great Plains Studies at the University of Nebraska – Lincoln describes the psychological challenges of the homestead years this way:

"Homesteading imposed peculiar, harsh, and extreme psychological demands on both men and women - single men, husbands, wives, widows, and single women. These were mostly poor people, especially during the first decade or so of their homesteading and for many extending much longer."

"Even when they did well, the sense or fear of failure haunted them. Most had no safety net at all, no substantial savings or health plan or retirement benefits or farm insurance, etc. Their whole existence depended on the enormous uncertainties of weather, insect or plant disease infestations, varying market prices, disabling accidents and sickness, childbirth, loss or crippling of draft animals, and more - none of which they themselves controlled."

"The stress of having one's life so dependent on luck or God's favor or whatever they believed did control these many risks must have been an ever-present burden, oppressive and deflating. [Interestingly, even today when farmers have many safety nets, rates of suicide, alcoholism, drug dependence, and depression are very high.]"

An article "About the Homestead Act" by the National Park Service has this summary:

"A filing fee was the only money required, but sacrifices and hard work extracted a different price from the hopeful settlers."[41]

One of the ever-present dangers in the pioneer era was the possibility of prairie fires that, without modern firefighting equipment, could spread unchecked for miles.

Homesteaders tried to beat out the flames with sacks or blankets doused with water. They also tried to stop fires with a plowed strip of land as a firebreak, hoping the flames wouldn't catch hold on the upturned earth and would self-extinguish.

In 1889, a massive grass fire was started during a drought by a settler who lit his pipe and then tossed the match into a manure pile, which smoldered until it erupted into a fire the next day. Fueled by winds gusting sixty to eighty miles an hour on April 2, the fire nearly decimated the town of Ree Heights and blazed a fiery swath through three counties.[42]

When it approached Buffalo County, H.J. Sinkie saw the smoke and flames racing toward his home and realized he'd have to stake his life on a patch of overturned dirt.

"The only hope of saving the lives of the family was on that small piece of plowing southwest of the house," he wrote.

"By this time, the fire was just a few rods from the house and as it was banked with dry manure and everything as dry as powder, I sprang into the house and carried the five children to the narrow strip of plowing and dragged some bed clothes to put over them. I also threw out a churn and tin covered trunk. By this time, flames were upon us. The heat was intense. My face and hands were badly singed. The children lay flat on the ground and never peeped."

Sinkie wrote that as the inferno burned around them while they cowered on their plowed plot on the prairie, he "watched our six years of hard earnings go up in smoke."[43]

His son Ernest, who was only about five or six years old when he faced the horror of the wall of fire, would later write, "I don't remember much about the blizzard of 1888, but the fire of 1889, I'll never forget!"[44]

Even though the strong winds rattled their house in the devastating 1888 "Children's Blizzard," the Sinkie family's home was snug and strong enough to withstand it as they huddled inside. But the fast moving and long lingering storm killed 500 people who were caught outdoors in freezing, white-out conditions or froze to death in a home that couldn't keep out the cold.

When the weather wasn't so dramatic, settlers could face vast emptiness and loneliness, especially in the early homesteading days when communities were just being established. In the country, there was often no one else and nothing else for miles.

Mrs. O.T. Dye described her first impression of central Dakota Territory as "one great stretch of prairie as far as you could see with once in awhile a claim shanty... ...I would not have known Gann Valley from any other part of the road if Trippet (her husband) hadn't told me. I think it had been the county seat for less than two months."[45]

There are even theories that the relentless wind itself, the only sound to break the often oppressive silence, may have contributed to feelings of loneliness and had a negative effect on settlers' mental health.

Under all of these conditions, people who had never displayed any sign of an inability to cope, were even feeling the strain and displaying unusual behavior.

In 1893, journalist Eugene Smalley wrote in a magazine article in *"The Atlantic"* that:

"an alarming amount of insanity occurs in the new prairie state among farmers and wives."

Smalley referenced the inherent dangers of winter in a drafty claim shanty that was hurriedly constructed to meet the Homestead Act requirement of building a dwelling on the land. He wrote:

"The silence of death rests on the vast landscape, save when it is swept by cruel winds that search out every chink and cranny of the buildings and drive through each unguarded aperture the dry, powdery snow."[46]

In addition, the homesteaders were virtually powerless against the epidemics that swept across the Plains: tuberculosis, cholera, smallpox, typhoid fever, diphtheria, scarlet fever and the Spanish flu.

Childbirth also was dangerous in the 1880's with the risk of hemorrhage or infection always looming before the invention of antibiotics. A doctor might be miles away, leaving the birthing process to midwives, sometimes just a neighbor to assist, and sometimes no one at all.

The estimated number of women who died in childbirth during the late 1800's in the United States was about five out of every thousand. Estimates from 1800 are that 462 in 1000 newborns did not survive infancy. By 1890, that number dropped by about half. Far better, but compare that to less than six infant deaths in 1000 births in 2025.

And even if they made it through infancy, more than 40 percent of children did not live to see their fifth birthday.[47]

Several years after Sarah was killed, the Kelley's daughter Maime and her baby would become one of those statistics. Maime lost her newborn child and her own life after she gave birth at home, leaving a husband and a little boy to mourn for them.

There's nothing more difficult for a parent than burying a child. Census records indicate that Dan and Sarah Kelley may have had as many as seven children, but only three survived.

By the end of the 19th century, Dan and Sarah Kelley had a terrible trifecta.

Loss.

Emotional strain.

Financial strain.

People react differently to extreme stress. Some find ways to cope. Some homesteaders in Buffalo County said that they joined together with their neighbors to hold spelling bees and dances to relax, distract and support each other.

But there are stories passed down through generations about other settlers who simply walked out into a blizzard to their death because they just couldn't take it anymore.

Symptoms of depression, withdrawal, changes in behavior and acting out through violence or suicide became well known enough on the Great Plains to earn names:[48]

Cabin fever.

Prairie fever.

Prairie madness.

Their own kind of epidemic. Long before post traumatic stress syndrome was ever diagnosed.

In the Kelley household, there were no incidents of violence before Dan turned the deed to the land over to Sarah. John testified at the trial that his parents hadn't even had significant arguments for most of their marriage and only began fighting when Dan wanted the deed to the land back.

And Dan and Sarah Kelley's modern descendants are some of the nicest, most mild-mannered people you'll ever meet.

So, what happened to Dan Kelley?

It's said that everyone has a breaking point.

If that is so, the prairie found Dan Kelley's.

And Dan Kelley snapped.

Women's Rights Of Land Ownership In the Homestead Days

Chapter 18

At a time when women were still of lower legal status than men, the fact that neighbors immediately stood up to report the suspicious nature of Sarah Kelley's death and testify about it was both a sign of the attitudes of an individual community and a sign of the times.

None of the neighbors who went to help after Sarah's death displayed any feeling that a man's wife was a man's property or was secondary as had been the case in some communities throughout history.

Remember H.J. Sinkie? When it appeared that his wife Bertha was on her deathbed during the typhoid epidemic, he prayed to God, "take anything, but save my wife."

Sarah Kelley's murder happened during a period of great change for women, fueled by the Homestead Act and the women's suffrage movement.

While single and widowed women were allowed to own property in their own name in the United States, married women did not have that right for much of the nation's first sixty to 100 years.

Up until almost the turn of the 20th century, married women could not own property in their own name and, if a single woman owned property, her ownership rights were largely transferred to her husband upon marriage under the legal principle of coverture.[49]

The Homestead Act of 1862 opened up land ownership in the new West to women who were single, widowed or "deserted."

A married woman could only stake a claim with the status as a "head of household" if her husband was incapacitated or unable to support the family.

A National Park Service - Nebraska article states that "Homesteading women created an atmosphere where ideas about women's rights could flourish. Historians have long acknowledged that the Homestead Act of 1862 was one of the most substantial and influential acts ever passed by Congress."[50]

But, even with attitudes toward women changing, allowing women to stake their 160 acres under the Homestead Act was also a practical matter.

America needed people to settle the West after the Louisiana Purchase. Lots of people. The purchase of more than 800,000 square miles of land from France in the Louisiana Purchase in 1803 had doubled the size of the nation with largely unsettled land.[51]

As many as four million people moved West to stake their claims and start their farms. Of those, more than 100,000 were women. In South Dakota, one out of every ten homesteaders was female, according to the South Dakota State Historical Society.[52]

Women homesteaders not only proved up their claims, they also proved themselves in rugged and inhospitable conditions.

Efforts to change the legal status of married women as landowners began before the Homestead Act went into effect, but it snowballed after the act became effective.

New York, which was also the birthplace of the women's suffrage movement in the 1840's, was the first state to allow married women to own property with the Married Women's Property Act of 1848.[53]

When South Dakota gained statehood in 1889, the new state constitution included a statute stating that married women could retain and attain separate property and would not be liable for the debts of her husband."[54]

That statute is what enabled Dan Kelley to transfer one quarter of land to Sarah Kelley.

By 1900, all states had legislation allowing married women to own property in their own name. But, although they could own land, women still didn't have the right to vote. They paid taxes on their land, which led to the suffrage campaign of "no taxation with representation," a rallying theme since the American Revolution when the American colonies won independence from England.[55]

Even though all states had laws allowing married women to own property in the 20th century, it would be 1920 before the United States ratified the 19th amendment, granting all American women the right to vote. Four states, Wyoming, Colorado, Idaho and Utah, had allowed women to vote by 1896. South Dakota passed a state amendment granting women the right to vote in the state in 1918.[56]

Note on the Spelling of the Name

The name Kelley has also been spelled Kelly at different points in the family history.

The spelling of Kelley is used in this book because that is the spelling based on census records. Kelley also was the primary spelling on John's military draft registration information. Kelly was noted on the draft registration as a secondary spelling.

Descendants say that after John moved out of Buffalo County, he went by Kelly because of the notoriety of the case.

The name was spelled Kelly on court documents from the case, which is why the newspapers at the time used that spelling in their coverage of the trial. However, in his death notice in *The Pioneer Press*, Dan's name was spelled as Kelley. Census records about Dan Kelley indicate that he could not read or write so he would not have been able to correct any misspellings.

The deciding factor in the use of the Kelley spelling was family information, John's draft documents and the fact that Kelley is how the name is spelled on Sarah's headstone.

Part 6

The Story Behind the Story

How the Book Came to Be

Author's Note

I heard about Sarah Kelley's murder when I was young, many years before I ever thought about writing this book.

My father was born and raised in Buffalo County just a few miles from the Kelley farm, albeit a few decades after Sarah Kelley was killed. I even lived in Gann Valley for a few months as a baby before my family moved away from Buffalo County.

Dad had heard about the case when he was growing up, but not all the details.

He mentioned it one day after we'd visited my grandmother and we were driving by Dan and Sarah Kelley's original homestead site. I asked what happened and he said all he knew was that she was beaten to death by her husband.

I remember how horrified he was by the thought that anyone would do that to his wife. My father worshipped my mother.

The Kelley case was filed in the back of my mind as another interesting piece of history in Buffalo County. Dad was full of stories about what life was like around Gann Valley when he was growing up.

I left South Dakota after college to pursue my career in news in Chicago at an international wire service and then in television news in Houston, Texas. As my parents grew older, my father asked me to move back home to be closer to them and help them.

When my father was in his nineties, I finally moved back for several years.

As we spent time together talking and reminiscing, I remembered the Buffalo County homestead murder case. Hmmm, I thought. That might make a good magazine article or a book if I could find out what happened.

Before I could start on it, my father was diagnosed with cancer. He underwent surgery and was hospitalized for six months in Sioux Falls. I moved from my parent's home to Sioux Falls so I could be with him all the time and make sure he had everything he needed.

While he recovered, we had lots of time to talk. I told him I wanted to find out more about the old murder case and asked if he knew if any of Sarah Kelley's family members were still around. He didn't know.

I asked if he knew where Sarah Kelley was buried. A cemetery would be a good place to start looking for answers. He said he didn't know where she was buried.

Then one day, he suddenly looked up from his hospital bed, turned to me and said, "She's at Duncan."

We weren't talking about the case at the time so I said, "What? Who?"

"Sarah Kelley," he said. "She's buried at Duncan."

The cemetery at St. Placidus Duncan Church. A cemetery I knew well because we had been going there to visit the graves of family members almost all my life.

I drove to Buffalo County and walked around the cemetery looking for a grave with Sarah Kelley's name on it. I didn't see one.

I decided to call the state's attorney. Buffalo County doesn't have its own prosecutor's office so I called State's Attorney Dedrich Koch in Wessington Springs, which is about 25 miles from Gann Valley, thinking that he might know about the case because he grew up near the church and the Kelley farm.

He didn't know about the case and wasn't a member of Duncan Church, but he suggested that I talk to my

Aunt Ellen Speck, who's a very active church member at Duncan.

I said, "That was my next call anyway!"

Ellen said Sarah's grave was the one in the far corner of the cemetery. I told her I hadn't seen a name on it and thought it was an unmarked grave. That's when I discovered it wasn't unmarked, but was positioned so the name was pointing into the evergreens that were planted years after her death. (The tombstone was turned around by Sarah Kelley's family after they learned where she was buried.)

She told me that the congregation found some details about the case when they were putting together a church history booklet for Duncan's 125th anniversary and suggested that I talk to Kathy Yost, who did their research on the case.

I talked to Kathy and looked at the booklet, which led me to Richard Sinkie, whose family had bought the land from John Kelley in 1919.

I was ready to dive into the details. I went to the courthouse and looked at the old documents with the trial testimony. It was all there: the murder, the motive and transcripts of testimony that would provide quotes from people who were witnesses in the trial.

Through their words, I could bring a century old murder case back to life. I tried to track down living descendants of Sarah Kelley by looking up records, but to no avail. Still, it was a good story without that element. And I knew there was a good chance that a relative would turn up and come forward after my article was published in *South Dakota Magazine*.

After the article was published, I checked my email and saw a message from my old high school classmate, Kim Joy Nelson. As it turns out, she was a descendant of John Kelley's wife Anna and so was Joe Fanning, who was also a classmate.

The answers had been all around all along, but they were hidden in a past that wasn't talked about and in a mystery that wasn't understood.

The missing pieces came together through my magazine article: the explanation of the whispers that Kim's mother heard at home with Anna and John and a tangible link to the victim through her grave.

The gravesite allowed the descendants to pay their respects to the mother of the man they knew as Grandpa John with an appreciation of the loss he had endured.

I was humbled and honored to help bring answers and closure.

As the layers of the story continued to unfold, I knew that this was going to make a good book, one that had begun just by talking to my dad when I was young and again when I was an adult.

My father was declining at this point. I kept him apprised of how the story was developing as I worked on it, told him details he had never known and showed him photos of Sarah Kelley's grave and the close-up photos of the remnants of the old Kelley house. He was excited that the article was coming to fruition.

He passed away a few months before the article was published, but I showed it to him before publication.

It gave us a final project to work on together. Something more to learn from the man who taught me everything from how to tie my shoes to how to check the oil in my car.

My mother, who met my father when she moved to South Dakota to teach school in Buffalo County, did get to see the article. To a woman who said she would have been wanted to be a newspaper editor if she hadn't become a teacher, it was an exciting project.

Mom didn't get to see the finished book, but she saw me working on it. I often thought of her and Dad as I wrote, thought of things they said about the case, about Duncan Church, and especially of how supportive they were and of how grateful I am to have had them in my life.

About the Author

and

Acknowledgements

About the Author

Award-winning journalist Sue Speck covered many high profile, big city crimes and trials as a television reporter in Houston, Texas. But she found a murder story equally as compelling in the tiny South Dakota cemetery where her family has visited the graves of relatives for decades.

Sue heard about the Sarah Kelley murder case because her father was born and raised in Buffalo County just a few miles from where it happened. While her dad only knew what he'd heard about the case while he was growing up, the 92-year-old gentleman was able to guide her to the answers.

In addition to working in television news, Sue also worked as a writer and editor on the national desk of an international news service in Chicago.

When she returned to South Dakota for several years to help her elderly parents, they talked about the case and Sue began investigating to find out what happened and why, which led to answers and closure for a family who had wondered what had led to the death of their great grandmother more than a century ago.

Some of the murder cases and trials that Sue has covered include the Andrea Yates multiple murder case, the Clara Harris murder case, and the railcar killer case.

Sue Speck is also the author of an authorized biography about the creator of Porter Sculpture Park in the book *The Power of the Bull: Inside the Head of Sculptor Wayne Porter,* which is an inspiring look at the sculptor's life, art and business journey.

Acknowledgements

This book would not have had the same heart without the parishioners of Duncan Church, people who have impressed me with their compassion for not only the victim of a century old murder, but for all the people who are buried in their small cemetery.

Through their services and fellowship at potluck dinners afterwards, they have shown me a sense of community that is extraordinary.

Specifically, I want to thank:

My Uncle Marvin's wife, Ellen Speck, who gave me information, encouragement, and Kathy Yost's phone number. Both provided contacts and immeasurable help along the way.

Kathy Yost, whose research into Sarah Kelley's murder during preparations for the church's 125th anniversary provided a head start for my investigation. She also provided contact information for some of Sarah Kelley's descendants who reached out to her after my article was published in South Dakota Magazine.

Kathy and I compared notes and shared research with each other to try to find more family members who had been wondering what happened in their family's past. Through her, I was able to contact more Kelley descendants and provide information to them.

I also want to thank:

The Brule County Clerk of Court's office for helping me locate old trial documents that gave me quotes from the trial testimony that brought a century old case to life.

The Buffalo County Register of Deeds office for guiding me to the land deeds.

Judy Gaulke, who directed me to other historic papers that provided information that had been lost from the court files.

The Pioneer Museum of Jerauld County for allowing me to look at newspapers from 1905.

The Miller Press for allowing me to look at newspapers from 1905 when *The Miller Press* was named *The Pioneer Press.*

The Hand County Library for providing access to other newspapers from 1905.

The Hand County Conservation Office for helping me look up soil information about Buffalo County.

The South Dakota Historical Society for providing access to historical information.

The Sinkie family: Richard for speaking with me and showing me the old homestead location and Lee Sinkie and Deb Morrison who helped me locate the deeds and transaction history for the deeds.

The descendants of Dan and Sarah Kelley, who shared their memories and thoughts of the tragedy that struck their family so many years ago.

I want to add here that the descendants I know would have been the last people I would have ever guessed had a connection to someone who had committed a homicide because they are some of the nicest and kindest people you'll ever meet.

I need to thank John Andrews at South Dakota Magazine for publishing my article about the Kelley murder case that brought everyone together.

And to my dear mother and father: I will be forever grateful for your love, wisdom and encouragement. Without you, none of the good that came out of this tragedy would have happened.

Endnotes

[1] Pioneer Experiences of H.J. Sinkie, History of Buffalo County 1885 – 1985, Gann Valley, South Dakota, Compiled by the Lady Helpers Society: Mrs. George Fraser, Mrs. C.C. Swartout, Mrs. C.G. Segar, Mrs. J.B. Ingerson, Mrs. Chris Krog, Bertha Krog, Dureene Petersen, Pearle I. Fraser, Ruth Viereck, Phyllis DeJong 1985

[2] Richard Maxwell Brown, The Enduring Frontier: The Impact of Weather on South Dakota History and Literature, 1985, South Dakota Historical Society Dunham Jerauld County p. 209-210, 218, 220-231, South Dakota 3:497, Kingsbury, Dakota Territory 2:1592; E. Frank Peterson comp., Historical Atlas of South Dakota (n.p. 1904 p. 178-179, Schell, Clay County p. 86

[3] "About the Homestead Act" National Park Service www.nps.gov/home/learn/history/culture/aboutthehomesteadact.htm

[4] Homesteading by the Numbers, National Historical Park, Nebraska, www.nps.gov/homes/learn/historyculture/bynubers.htm

[5] Drawn to the Land, South Dakota Historical Society, www.history.gov/museum/docs/Homesteading South Dakota

[6] Pioneer Experiences of H.J. Sinkie, History of Buffalo County 1885 – 1985, Gann Valley, South Dakota,

Compiled by the Lady Helpers Society: Mrs. George Fraser, Mrs. C.C. Swartout, Mrs. C.G. Segar, Mrs. J.B. Ingerson, Mrs. Chris Krog, Bertha Krog, Dureene Petersen, Pearle I. Fraser, Ruth Viereck, Phyllis DeJong 1985

[7] Allyson Brooks and Steph Jaco, Homesteading and Agricultural Development Context, 1994, South Dakota State Historical Center, Vermillion, SD. South Dakota Historical Society www.history.sd.gov/preservation/docs/HomesteadAgDevlop.pdf

[8] Homesteading, South Dakota State Historical Society, www.history.sd.gov/musuem /docs/Homesteading.pdf

[9] Treaty of Fort Laramie (1868), National Archives, https://archives.gov/milestone-documents-fort-laramie-treaty

[10] Homesteading, South Dakota State Historical Society, www.history.sd.gov/musuem /docs/Homesteading.pdf

[11] Thomas Witt, Kathleen Corbett, Holly Norton, James Steely, The History of Agriculture in South Dakota: Components for a Fully Developed Historic Context, SWCA Environmental Consultants, July 2013,

www.history.sd.gov/preservation/docs/SDAgricultureContext2013.pdf

[12] Richard Maxwell Brown, The Enduring Frontier: The Impact of Weather on South Dakota History and Literature, 1985, South Dakota Historical Society

[13] History of Buffalo County 1885 – 1985, Gann Valley, South Dakota, Compiled by the Lady Helpers Society: Mrs. George Fraser, Mrs. C.C. Swartout, Mrs. C.G. Segar, Mrs. J.B. Ingerson, Mrs. Chris Krog, Bertha Krog, Dureene Petersen, Pearle I. Fraser, Ruth Viereck, Phyllis DeJong 1985

[14] Paula M. Nelson, Everything I Want is Here!: The Dakota Farmers' Rural Ideal, 1884-1934 p. 108, www.sdhspress.com/journal/south-dakota-history-22-2/everything-i-want-is-here-the-dakota-rural-farmers-rural-ideal=1884-1934/vol-22-no-2-everything-i-want-is-here.pdf   Schell, History of South Dakota, p. 343-344, Robinson, History of South Dakota p. 153.

[15] Allyson Brooks and Steph Jaco, Homesteading and Agricultural Development Context, 1994, South Dakota State Historical Center, Vermillion, SD, South Dakota Historical Society (Schell 1975:344)

[16] The Children's Blizzard in the Black Hills Country, National Weather Service, www.weather.gov/unr1888-01012

The Children's Blizzard, Jan 2013 South Dakota Historical Foundation www.sdhsf.org/news_events/history_articles.html/title/january-2013-the-children's-blizzard

Pioneer Days of H.J. Sinkie, History of Buffalo County 1885 – 1985, Gann Valley, South Dakota, Compiled by the Lady Helpers Society: Mrs. George Fraser, Mrs. C.C. Swartout, Mrs. C.G. Segar, Mrs. J.B. Ingerson, Mrs. Chris Krog, Bertha Krog, Dureene Petersen, Pearle I. Fraser, Ruth Viereck, Phyllis DeJong 1985

[17] Richard Maxwell Brown, The Enduring Frontier: The Impact of Weather on South Dakota History and Literature, 1985, South Dakota Historical Society

[18] Thomas Witt, Kathleen Corbett, Holly Norton, James Steely, The History of Agriculture in South Dakota: Components for a Fully Developed Historic Context, SWCA Environmental Consultants, July 2013, www.history.sd.gov/preservation/docs/SDAgricultureContext2013.pdf

[19] Thomas Witt, Kathleen Corbett, Holly Norton, James Steely, The History of Agriculture in South Dakota: Components for a Fully Developed Historic Context, SWCA Environmental Consultants, July 2013, www.history.sd.gov/preservation/docs/SDAgricultureContext2013.pdf

[20] From National Weather Service and National Oceanic and Atmospheric Administration records.
This Day in Weather History, National Weather Service, www.weather.gov/abr/This_Day_in_Weather_HIstory_Feb_12

[21] Quotes on pages 18 to 25 are from trial testimony from Buffalo County, SD court documents, 1905.

[22] Information and quotes from page 26 to page 27 are from court documents: Trial testimony of Dr. Clara McManus. Buffalo County Court, 1905

[23] Murder or Suicide Dan Kelly (sic) Charged With Murder of his Wife, March 2, 1905 The Pioneer Press, Miller SD

[24] Murder South of Us! Daniel Kelly (sic) in Buffalo County Charged with Killing His Wife, Miller Sun 1905

[25] Duncan Doings, March 2, 1905 The Dakota Chief, Gann Valley, SD

[26] Held for Murder Dan Kelly Charged with the Horrible Crime of Wife Murder, March 2, 1905 The Dakota Chief, Gann Valley, SD

[27] Held for Murder Dan Kelly Charged with the Horrible Crime of Wife Murder, March 2, 1905 The Dakota Chief, Gann Valley, SD

[28] Held for Murder Dan Kelly Charged with the Horrible Crime of Wife Murder, March 2, 1905 The Dakota Chief, Gann Valley, SD

[29] Found Guilty Daniel Kelly convicted for Wife Murder Received a Life Sentence, July 20, 1905, The Dakota Chief, Gann Valley, SD

[30] Women Homesteaders and Suffrage, Homestead National Historical Park Nebraska, www.nps.gov/home/homesteading-and-suffrage.htm

[31] South Dakota State Constitution Article 21-5, www.sdsos.gov/2023SouthDakotaConstitution20220124.pdf

[32] Testimony from page 34 to page 47 from trial testimony from Buffalo County, SD court documents, 1905.

[33] Found Guilty Daniel Kelly Convicted for Wife Murder Received a Life Sentence, July 20, 1905, The Dakota Chief, Gann Valley, SD

[34] Found Guilty Daniel Kelly Convicted for Wife Murder Received a Life Sentence, July 20, 1905, The Dakota Chief, Gann Valley, SD

[35] Found Guilty Daniel Kelly Convicted for Wife Murder Received a Life Sentence, July 20, 1905, The Dakota Chief, Gann Valley, SD

[36] Found Guilty Daniel Kelly Convicted for Wife Murder Received a Life Sentence, July 20, 1905, The Dakota Chief, Gann Valley, SD

[37] A Life Sentence, July 27, 1905, The Pioneer Press, Miller, SD

[38] (Special Report to the Argus Leader) Evidence of Brutal Crime Testimony Bought Out Startling Facts Pleases Buffalo County General Sentiment is that Old Man Deserves Life Sentence, July 24, 1905, Argus Leader, Sioux Falls, SD

[39] July 27 1911, Pioneer Press, Miller, SD

[40] St. Placidus Parish 125th Anniversary, Duncan Catholic Church "Little Church on the Prairie" 2012 History complied by Ellen Speck and Kathy Yost

[41] About the Homestead Act, National Park Service www.nps.gov/home/learn/history/culture/aboutthehomesteadact.htm

[42] Richard Maxwell Brown, The Enduring Frontier: The Impact of Weather on South Dakota History and Literature, 1985, South Dakota Historical Society

Scott Heidepriem, Bring on the Pioneers: History of Hand County (Pierre SD: State Publishing Co 1978, p 56-57, Dunham, Jerauld County p 342-345
Federal Writers Project, South Dakota p 262

[43] Pioneer Days of H.J. Sinkie, History of Buffalo County 1885 – 1985, Gann Valley, South Dakota, Compiled by the Lady Helpers Society: Mrs. George Fraser, Mrs. C.C. Swartout, Mrs. C.G. Segar, Mrs. J.B. Ingerson, Mrs. Chris Krog, Bertha Krog, Dureene Petersen, Pearle I. Fraser, Ruth Viereck, Phyllis DeJong 198

[44] Ernest Sinkie, History of Buffalo County 1885 – 1985, Gann Valley, South Dakota, Compiled by the Lady Helpers Society: Mrs. George Fraser, Mrs. C.C. Swartout, Mrs. C.G. Segar, Mrs. J.B. Ingerson, Mrs. Chris Krog, Bertha Krog, Dureene Petersen, Pearle I. Fraser, Ruth Viereck, Phyllis DeJong 1985

[45] Early Experiences of Mrs. O.T. Dye, History of Buffalo County 1885 – 1985, Gann Valley, South Dakota, Compiled by the Lady Helpers Society: Mrs. George Fraser, Mrs. C.C. Swartout, Mrs. C.G. Segar, Mrs. J.B. Ingerson, Mrs. Chris Krog, Bertha Krog, Dureene

Petersen, Pearle I. Fraser, Ruth Viereck, Phyllis DeJong 1985

[46] E.V. Smalley, The Isolation of Life on Prairie Farms, The Atlantic, 9-1893, www.theatlantic.com/magazine/archives/1893/09/the-isolation-on-the-prairie-farmers/523959

[47] Deaths in Childbed from the Eighteenth Century to 1935, National Institutes of Health, Jan. 30, 1986, ww.pubmed.ncbi.nlm.nih.gov/3511335

The First Measured Century: Infant Mortality and Life Expectancy, PBS, www.pbs.org/fmc/timeline/dmortality.htm

[48] James Gaines, Is the Silence of the Great Plains to Blame for Prairie Madness, July 22, 2022, AtlasObscura, www.atlassobscura.com/articles/prairie-madness-study-silence-great-plains

Matt W. Wolff, Too Little House on the Verge of Prairie Madness, Aug. 16, 2020, Psychology Today www.psychologytoday.com/us/blog/strifes-rich-pageant/202008/too-little-house-the-verge-prairie-madness

[49] Coverture: The Word You Probably Don't Know But Should, Sept. 4, 2012, Women's History, https://www.womenshistory.org/articles/coverture-word-you-probably-dont-know-should

[50] Women Homesteaders and Suffrage, Homestead National Historical Park Nebraska, www.nps.gov/home/homesteading-and-suffrage.htm

[51] National Archives and Records Administration, www.archives.gov/exhibits/american_originals/loupurch.html

[52] Women Homesteaders, National Historical Park – Nebraska, National Park Service, www.nps.gov/home/learn/history/culture/women-homesteaders.htm

[53] Women's Rights: Dress Reform, Property Rights, and More, Susan B. Anthony Museum, www.susanb.org/womens-rights

[54] South Dakota State Constitution Article 21-5, www.sdsos.gov/2023SouthDakotaConstitution20220124.pdf

www.sdlegislature.gov/constitution/21-5

[55] Women Homesteaders and Suffrage: Planted in the Soil, National Historical Park Nebraska, National Park Service, www.nps.gov/home/homesteading-and-suffrage.htm

[56] Women's Suffrage in the Progressive Era, The Library of Congress, https//www.loc.gov>classroom-materials/united-states-history-primary-source-timeline/progressive-era-to-new-era-1900

www.ingramcontent.com/pod-product-compliance
Lightning Source LLC
LaVergne TN
LVHW022232080526
838199LV00105B/241